Spelling

John Butterworth

Illustrations by Lee Nicholls

OXFORD

UNIVERSITY PRESS

OXFORD
UNIVERSITY PRESS

Great Clarendon Street, Oxford OX2 6DP

Oxford University Press is a department of the University of Oxford.
It furthers the University's objective of excellence in research, scholarship,
and education by publishing worldwide in

Oxford New York

Auckland Bangkok Buenos Aires
Cape Town Chennai Dar es Salaam Delhi Hong Kong Istanbul
Karachi Kolkata Kuala Lumpur Madrid Melbourne Mexico City Mumbai
Nairobi São Paulo Shanghai Taipei Tokyo Toronto

Oxford is a registered trade mark of Oxford University Press
in the UK and in certain other countries

British Library Cataloguing in Publication Data available

ISBN 0-19-911158-8

1 3 5 7 9 10 8 6 4 2

Designed and Typeset by Mike Brain Graphic Design Limited
Printed in Hong Kong

Contents

Sounds

Human language is a language of sounds. The sounds are made with the voice, like this:

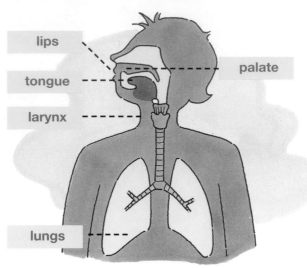

lips

palate

tongue

larynx

lungs

Air pushed up from the lungs makes a vibrating sound
The mouth 'shapes' the sound, using the lips, tongue and the palate

In the word *bat* you can hear three sounds, **b**, **a**, and **t**.
Look in a mirror and see how your mouth changes to make each one.

....

Letters

are signs for sounds. They are used to spell words.

All the letters together are called the alphabet – after the first two letters in the ancient Greek language: *alpha*, α and *beta*, β

This is the English alphabet:

a b c d e f g h i j k l m n o p q r s t u v w x y z

....

Phonemes

Sounds like **b**, **a** and **t** are called **phonemes**. Phonemes are the smallest bits of sound you can split a word into.

Splitting a word into phonemes can help you to spell it.

phonemes	spelling
h i t	*hit*
r u n	*run*
s t o p	*stop*

bat, *hit*, *run* and *stop* are easy words to spell.
They have one letter for each phoneme.

Sounds of English

All the different phonemes of English are shown here.
They are printed in colour.

Try saying all these phonemes aloud, to hear the sounds – *a ee* . . . *p* etc.

a in *bad*	**e** in *bed*	**i** in *in*	**o** in *on*
oo in *wood*	**u** in *sun*	**er** in *water*	

ee in *see*	**ear** in *hear*	**ai** in *rain*	**air** in *hair*
or in *for*	**oo** in *moon*	**oor** in *poor*	**ar** in *car*
oa in *boat*	**oy** in *boy*	**ir** in *girl*	
ou in *out*		**ie** in *tie*	

What is the difference between the red phonemes and the blue ones?
You can find out on the next page.

p in *put*	**b** in *but*	**t** in *to*	**d** in *do*
k in *kick*	**g** in *go*	**f** in *four*	**v** in *five*
m in *make*	**n** in *name*	**ng** in *sing*	**h** in *him*
s in *so*	**z** in *zoo*	**y** in *yes*	**w** in *wet*
l in *like*	**th** in *then*	**th** in *three*	**r** in *run*
ch in *chip*	**sh** in *ship*	**j** in *jump*	**si** in *television*

As you can *hear*, there are 44 different phonemes; and, as you can see, there are only 26 letters! That is why some phonemes need more than one letter to spell them, like the **sh** sound in *shout* or the **ng** sound in *sing*.

Accent

Not everyone speaks in the same way. The different ways of saying words are called accents. Your accent depends mostly on where you live, or where you learnt to speak English. Facts about accent have this sign next to them:

Vowels

Vowels are the phonemes you get when the air comes out freely, and nothing blocks its way. In this book vowel sounds are shown in red.

oo ar and *ee* are all vowel sounds. Say them in front of a mirror, and watch – and feel – what happens.

oo ar ee: who's saying which?

The single letters that spell vowels are a e i o u and *sometimes* y:

bag   beg   big   bog   bug   buggy

But many of the vowel sounds in English are spelt by two or more letters:

say   growl   snarl   shout   hoot   scream   sigh

Consonants

Consonants are sounds that are made by blocking parts of the mouth with the lips, tongue or teeth, so that the air-stream is stopped or slowed down. In this book consonant sounds are printed in blue.

Here are some consonant sounds. Try them:

p and *b* stop the air with the lips, then let it out in a rush.
t and *d* do the same with the tongue.
r and *v* and *w* leave a small gap, to make a vibrating sound.
s and *sh* leave a small gap to make a hissing sound.
m and *n* and *ng* block the mouth and send the air out through the nose.

The letters that spell consonants are

b c d f g h j k l m n p q r s t v w x z and *sometimes* *y*

Long and short vowels

Vowel sounds are divided into two main groups – long and short.

Say these words:

pat   pet   pit   pot   put   but

The vowels in these words are called **short vowels** because they *sound* short.

All other vowel sounds are **long**, for example in these words:

pale	*feel*	*smile*	*goal*
rule	*boil*	*fall*	*me*

Can you hear the difference?

Consonant clusters

Consonants can be put together to make **clusters**:

s + k *skip*   **m + p** *jump*   **s + p + r** *spring*

Here are some more consonant cluster spellings. Find some words that *begin* with them.

cr   pl   thr   str

List some words which *end* with these clusters

nd   nk   lf   st   (You can use a dictionary to help you find words.)

Sly -y-

y- at the beginning of a word is always a consonant:

yet   yes   yesterday   you   yours   yawn   yellow

At the end of a word, **-y** is a vowel.

It can be a **short** vowel   *happy   sunny   pony   twenty   early*
or a **long** vowel   *cry   fly   why   my   try   spy*

Syllables

A syllable is a block of sound that makes up one beat in a word.

animal has **3** syllables:	*an - i - mal*
hamster has **2** syllables:	*ham - ster*
hippopotamus has **5** syllables:	*hip - po - pot - a - mus*
caterpillar has **4** syllables:	*cat - er - pil - lar*
cat has **1** syllable:	*cat*

Say these words aloud, and tap once for each syllable.

Many of the words in the English language are one-syllable words:

cat   dog   stop   go   in   out   laugh   cry

Sometimes you can find one-syllable words in the spelling of longer words:

cat in *caterpillar*   *hip* and *pot* in *hippopotamus*   *ham* in *hamster*

But most syllables are not words: they are just parts of words:

-er   -ster   -pil-   -lar   -mus

....

Syllable sounds

A syllable can be a vowel sound on its own:
i   a   er

But syllables are usually a mixture of consonants and vowels:
an   mal   hip   po   pot   mus   ster   cat

Parts of a syllable

Many syllables can be divided into two parts – **onset** and **rime**.

If a syllable has a consonant, or a consonant cluster, before the vowel it is called the **onset**. The word *onset* means *beginning*.

must	*most*	*missed*	all have the same onset: *m*
stop	*start*	*sting*	all have the same onset: *st*

Think of some one-syllable words which have the same onsets as

play   *cheat*   *spring*

The rest of the syllable, including the vowel, is called the **rime**.
The rime is the part that makes one syllable *rhyme* with another:

must	*just*	*trust*	all have the same rime: *ust*
stop	*top*	*flop*	all have the same rime: *op*
play	*stay*	*may*	all have the same rime: *ay*

Did you notice that **ay** is just a vowel sound? There is no consonant after it.

Some syllables have no *onset*.

What is the rime in these three words?   *arm*   *farm*   *harm*
Which one has no onset?

Which of these has no onset?   *ledge*   *sledge*   *edge*

Listening for rime and onset can often help you to spell new words, using words you know already:

sharp, park ⇨ *shark*   **hide, edge** ⇨ *hedge*
crisp, must ⇨ *crust*   **street, main** ⇨ *strain*

Spell the word for a dog's bark that has an onset like *you* and a rime like *help*.

Words sounds with meaning

What makes words different from other sounds is **meaning**.

Some words have just one bit of meaning; some are *formed* from smaller bits of meaning put together.

Knowing what words mean, and how words are formed, can help you to spell them.

Simple words and Compound words

Simple words are words with just one bit of meaning:

sun   water   wood   house   light   land   fall

But many English words are formed by putting two simple words together. These are called **compound words**:

sun + light ⇨ sunlight   wood + land ⇨ woodland
water + fall ⇨ waterfall   light + house ⇨ lighthouse

If you can spell the simple words, it's easy to spell the *compound* word.

Can you see the   words in these **compound** words?

skateboard   motorcycle   steamroller   hovercraft
inside   overtake   upright   throughout

Prefixes and suffixes

A lot of words in English have bits fixed on. These are not whole words, but they can change the meaning of a word, or the way it is used.

For example, **un-** fixed on the front of a word can make it mean the opposite:

fair ⇨ unfair   usual ⇨ unusual

Bits can be fixed on the end of a word, too, like the ending **-ly**:

fair ⇨ fairly   usual ⇨ usually.

Parts added in front of a word are called **prefixes**.
Parts added to the end of a word are called **suffixes**.

The part to which prefixes or suffixes are added is called the **root**.
If the root is a complete word (like *fair* or *usual*), it is called the **root word**.

Spelling words

In some languages each sound has the same spelling every time. Not in English!

For example, the vowel sound **or** in *for* can be spelt in all these ways:

-or- -ore- -au- -aw- -a- . . . and *more*. (See page 20)

The good news is that most words come in sets that have the same sound and the same spelling:

more sore* bore core score adore ignore ...
all ball call fall stall tall wall hall small ...

The trick is to learn the words in sets and not one at a time. Words which don't belong to large sets – the odd ones out – have to be learnt and remembered separately.
For example:

 saw* jaw claw

haul maul   *crawl shawl trawl sprawl*

The sign means that these words have unusual spellings.

Homophones

Homophone means *sounds the same*. Homophones are *words* that have the same sound, but different meanings. They may also have different spellings.

On this page *sore* and *saw* are homophones. If there are two homophones on the same page they are marked with a *. With homophones you have to remember the spelling together with the meaning.

Some more examples of homophones are:

pear pair   *one won*   *two to too*   *sail sale*

A good way to learn the spelling of a word is to *look* at it and *say* it, *cover* it with a piece of card or another book, *write* it from memory, then look at it again to *check*.

It is also a good idea when you say it to put it in a short phrase to show its meaning – just in case it is a homophone.

won	*'won the race'*		*won*	*won* ✔
LOOK	SAY	COVER	WRITE	CHECK

Spelling Short Vowels

In English there are six **short vowels** *a e i o u oo*

You can hear them in the middle of one-syllable words, like:

tip   top   tap   *bet   but   put*

hot dog
short vowel **o**

hot	*dog*	*lost*	*hop*	*hopping*	*hotter*
spot	*log*	*cost*	*stop*	*stopping*	*spotter*

fat cat
short vowel **a**

fat	*fatter*	*sad*	*happy*	*man*	*frantic*
cat	*batter*	*bad*	*snappy*	*can*	*gigantic*

big fish
short vowel **i**

big	*chip*	*think*	*win*	*winner*	*wishing*
twig	*skip*	*stink*	*spin*	*dinner*	*fishing*

red hen
short vowel **e**

hen	*better*	*bend*	*red*	*best*	*jelly*
ten	*letter*	*send*	*shed*	*test*	*smelly*

mucky duck
short vowel **u**

fun	*funny*	*duck*	*rust*	*rusty*	*butter*
sun	*sunny*	*muck*	*dust*	*dusty*	*gutter*

looking good

short vowel **oo**

good wood hood stood   foot soot   wool room
book took cook look rook shook crook

 Not everyone says these words in the same way.
Some people give them a long vowel, like the **oo** in *pool* and *cool*.
How do you say them?

....

Same sound – different spelling

These have the short vowel **e**:

dead	bread	ready	feather	healthy	measure	deaf
head	tread	steady	weather	wealthy	pleasure	sweat

 So do these: said   friend   leisure   any   many

The vowel sound in these words is **o**, but it's spelt with an **-a-**:

want watch wand wander waddle twaddle
swan swallow swap swamp wash squash

Do you notice anything about the **onsets** of all these words (i.e. the consonants in front of the vowel)?

These words have the same vowel sounds as *fun* and *sun* but look how they are spelt:

won	one	money	come	tongue	love	other
son	done	honey	some	among	glove	mother
ton	none				above	brother
						another

 And these   young double trouble   flood blood

These have a short **oo** but are spelt with a **-u-**: put push bush pull full

 In a lot of accents the single vowel **-u-** *always* has an **oo** sound, so that *but* rhymes with *put*, and *rush* rhymes with *push*. Do they rhyme when you say them, or not?

 Three important **oo** words: would should could

Spelling Long Vowels

By doubling letters, or putting different letters together, lots of other vowel sounds can be made, most of which are **long vowels**:

ee ie ai air oa oo or ow . . . etc.

From here to page 21 is all about spelling long vowels.

free wheel
the long vowel **ee**

double -e spells a vowel called **long -e** or **ee**. You can hear it in these words:

*meet**	*steep*	*free*	*seed*	*eel*	*week**
feet	*weep*	*tree*	*weed*	*feel*	*seek*
greet	*sheep*	*agree*	*deed*	*steel*	*cheek*
sheet	*creep*	*referee*	*speed*	*wheel*	

and in these:

breeze sneeze freeze squeeze cheese fleece sleeve

bean feast
Another way to spell **ee** is **-ea-**:

meal	*mean*	*eat*	*each*	*east*	*weak**
steal	*bean*	*meat**	*teach*	*feast*	*speak*
deal	*clean*	*treat*	*reach*	*beast*	*sneak*
seal		*wheat*		*yeast*	*streak*

tea	*leave*	*ease*	*leaf*	*peace*
flea	*heave*	*please*	*sheaf*	

In these **ee** is spelt with single **-e**:

she me he we be

and in: *lever fever cedar Peter*

chief thief

In front of an **f** the **ee** sound is often spelt **-ie-**:

chief   thief   grief   belief   relief   handkerchief   mischief

Also watch for: *piece*   *niece*   *field*   *shield*   *shriek*

 *receive   deceive   ceiling   seize*   What's different about these words?

All on their own: *people   police*

Lots of homophones have the long vowel **ee** in them:

meet	*steel*	*heel*	*bee*	*been*	*piece*
meat	*steal*	*heal*	*be*	*bean*	*peace*

tears and fears
the long vowel **ear**

These words all have the same *rime*, and it's spelt **-ear**:

ear   fear   tear   year   near   spear   clear   gear   hear*   appear

But in some words the spelling is **-eer**:

cheer   beer   peer*   sheer   sneer   queer

weird   weir   pier*

 *here*   sphere   mere   sincere*

far star
the long vowel **ar**

far	*arm*	*start*	*hard*	*park*	*sharp*
star	*farm*	*part*	*card*	*dark*	*harp*

 *calm   palm*   *aunt*   *father*

 Some people also say these words with the long vowel **ar**:

bath   past   plant   faster   after   nasty   . . . but not everyone.

How do you say them: With a short **a** like *cat*, or a long **ar** like *cart*?

-e on the end

makes it *long*

Hundreds of English words end in **-e**.
In most of them the **-e** is *silent*.

Say:

name	*hide*	*hope*	*tube*	*made*	*wipe*
game	*wide*	*rope*	*cube*	*fade*	*stripe*
shame	*stride*	*microscope*		*lemonade*	*type*

The **-e** has no sound itself, but it can still make a difference to the syllable. If the vowel before it is a *single* one, the **-e** usually makes it *long*.

mad ⇨ *made*   *hid* ⇨ *hide*   *tub* ⇨ *tube*
strip ⇨ *stripe*   *hop* ⇨ *hope*   *cub* ⇨ *cube*

Say these syllables aloud:

gat	*hol*	*driv*	*chim*	*whit*
siz	*wav*	*tast*	*phon*	*jok*

Then make them into words by adding an **-e** on the end.

How have the vowel sounds changed?
The **-e** wasn't always silent. In the Middle Ages words like *name* had two syllables, with a vowel sound at the end. In those days *name* would probably have rhymed with our word *farmer*.

 A few words that end in **-e** keep their *short* vowels:

gone	*one*	*some*	*love*	*have*
shone	*done*	*come*	*dove*	

Lots of different consonants can go between the vowel and the **e**:
a☐e   **o☐e**   **i☐e** *etc.*

long face, long tail
the long vowel *ai*

tail	pain	rail	aim	wait*
snail	brain	fail	claim	bait
chain	sail*			

The vowel in *face* is also long. It's the **-e** that makes it long.

ate	take	pale	ace	waste	same
gate	make	gale	place	taste	tame
hate	wake	sale*	face	paste	blame
plate	mistake	stale	grace	haste	game

Try finding some more **a□e** words.

 But also remember these tricky ones: *great   break   steak   straight   weight**

At the end of a word or syllable, this vowel is usually spelt **-ay**:

say   may   day   away   tray   way*   play   pray*

 But look out for: *they   grey   obey   prey**
  weigh*   sleigh   neighbour

fair hair
the long vowel *air*

Here are some of the words that have this vowel:

air   hair   fair   pair   chair   repair   despair

fare   stare   hare   care   mare   dare   bare*   glare
rare   square   scare   compare   beware   declare

 wear   tear   bear*   pear
  where   there

cool pool
the long vowel **oo**

pool	loop	soon	boot	roof	zoo
fool	hoop	moon	root	proof	too*
stool	scoop	spoon	shoot	hoof	tattoo
cool		afternoon			igloo
school					shoo!*

Some double **-o** words end in **-e**:

loose goose moose   choose groove

oo can also be spelt **-ue-**:

glue true blue argue cue value continue due*

or **u☐e**:

cute brute flute tune use fuse rude include fortune

It can also be spelt **-ew-**:

chew screw new crew dew* few threw* newt

 cruise bruise   prove move
lose you shoe*
view queue through* do

Don't forget the terrible *two*some, or *three*some, *to*   *too*   *two*

An **r** after this vowel produces **oor**, as in

poor moor
sure cure pure manure   tour

Have you noticed that in some of the words on this page there's a **y** sound before the vowel? Try to find out when this happens and when it doesn't.

go slow
the long vowel *oa*

At the end of a word this long vowel is spelt with a single **-o**:

no go so piano tomato potato ago also banjo

But it can also be spelt **-ow-**:

*low snow show blow glow flow throw
know below follow tow**

Before consonants it's likely to be **-oa-**:

oats	*oak*	*road*	*coal*	*coast*	*coach*
boats	*soak*	*toad*	*foal*	*boast*	*poach*
goats	*cloak*		*goal*	*toast*	

or **o☐e**:

pole	*poke*	*globe*	*rode*	*rose*	*note*
stole	*spoke*	*robe*	*code*	*nose*	*wrote*
hole	*joke*		*explode*	*those*	*vote*

In these words the **-o-** is long, too:
*old bold sold gold hold fold told
roll stroll   most ghost   won't don't*

 toe* doe though oh

boil in oil
the long vowel *oi*

You can hear the sound *oi* in:

*oil boil coil foil toil coin join point
boiler toilet noise voice choice poison*

But at the end of a word or syllable it's spelt **-oy**:

boy toy annoy destroy loyal royal voyage

 oyster

loud cow

the long vowel **ou**

Listen for the vowel sound in these words, spelt **-ow-**:

how   now   cow   bow   wow!
brown   town   frown   crown   drown
owl   howl   growl   prowl   scowl

towel   vowel
How are these two different?

It can also be spelt **-ou-**:

out	*loud*	*count*	*fountain*
spout	*cloud*	*amount*	*mountain*
about			

house   mouse
How are these two different?

 And occasionally **-ough**:

plough   bough

With an **-r** added, the vowel becomes **our**:

our   hour   sour   flour*

not to be confused with:

flower*   shower   power   tower

short horse

the long vowel **or**

The phoneme **or** is usually spelt **-or-**:

or	*corn*	*short*	*lord*	*pork*	*horse*	*force*
for	*horn*	*sport*	*ford*	*fork*	*gorse*	
	worn	*report*	*record*	*cork*		

But how many other ways of spelling it can you see?

sore   more   wore   door   floor   hoard   board
claw   paw   pawn   prawn   dawn   drawn
cause   pause   clause   applause   autumn   August   fraud
ought   fought   bought   thought
caught   taught   daughter   talk   walk   stalk
all   call   fall   wall   tall   also   water
wart   ward   towards   reward

 broad   four

fly high
the long vowel **ie**

This vowel has several spellings:

-y: *my* *by* *fly* *try* *sty*

-ie: *die* *lie* *tie*

-i☐e:

line	*pipe*	*pile*	*ice*	*wise*	*white*
fine	*ripe*	*mile*	*price*	*size*	*quite*
mine	*stripe*	*smile*	*nice*	*prize*	*polite*

Followed by **-t**, it is often spelt **-igh-**:

might *light* *fight* *fright* *bright* *night* *sight* *slight*

height   And don't forget: *I* *high* *eye*

either   *neither*

Some people say *either* and *neither* with **ee**

whirly bird
the long vowel **ir**

Which vowel sound can you hear in all these words?

fir	*girl*	*dirt*	*bird*	*firm*	*first*	*circle*
stir	*whirl*	*skirt*	*third*	*squirm*	*thirst*	

turn *burn* *burst* *church* *hurt* *curve* *fur*
turtle *hurtle* *turkey* *burger* *murder*

her *herd** *verb* *verse* *germ* *term* *stern* *certain* *person*

See if you can add some more words to each group.

These words have the **ir** phoneme in them but the spelling is **-or-**:

word *worm* *work* *worse* *worst*

How else are these five words alike?

Here are some more odd ones: *earn* *learn* *heard** *early* *were*

Spelling Consonants

Most consonants are easy to spell. You hear the sound and you write the letter. But sometimes there is more than one way to spell a consonant.

From here to page 27 is all about spelling consonants.

....

Doubles

Many words have double consonants, after short vowels and before endings like **-y**, **-le**, **-ing**, **-er**, **-est**, **-ed** … etc.:

happy   matter   sunny   bottle   bobbing   jogging   yellow

In English, double consonants don't sound any different from single ones, but they can make a difference to the vowel in front of them. For example: *matter* rhymes with *batter*, but if it had one **t** it would rhyme with *later* and *waiter*.

Listen to the difference between

hopping – hoping   bonny – bony   bitter – biter   supper – super

How do you think these words would sound if the double letter was single?

sloppy   copper   happen   bigger

There is more about doubling consonants on page 29.

Watch out for **s**, **f** and **l** doubling at the *ends* of words. They are usually one-syllable words, with *single* vowels:

Nasty Whiff

toss   loss   cross   mess   dress   less   miss   hiss mass   glass   fuss

 this   bus   thus   gas   plus

fluff   puff   gruff   off   cliff   stiff   whiff   scruff 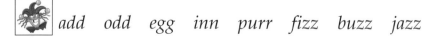 *if*

all   ball   call   fall   bell   well   tell   sell will   grill   thrill   pill   roll   stroll

Most of the other consonants are single when they come at the end. But make a note of these ones:

add   odd   egg   inn   purr   fizz   buzz   jazz

Silent letters

In many words there are consonant letters that have no sound:

know knife knee knock knot
gnat gnaw sign design
half calf calm palm
walk talk chalk
would could should
rustle trestle thistle
write wrote wreck wrap wrong

Which letters are silent in these groups of words?
Try to add some more words to each group.

Listen to the difference between these words . . .
scene science scissors ascend descend
. . . and these:
rescue scarf scrape escape telescope
What is the difference?

-gh-

The letters **-gh-** appear in lots of words, and it is hard to see why they are there.

sight fight tight night fright slight right
high sigh thigh   weigh sleigh neigh
thought fought ought nought bought
caught taught daughter slaughter
thorough borough   through   although

wh-

Many words begin with **wh-**. But the **-h-** is almost silent.

where when why what while
whale wheel white whisper whistle whopper

 What's silent in these three?
who whose whole

juggling giant
consonants **g** and **j**

The letter **g** has two sounds. One is 'hard', and it is always spelt **-g-** or **-gg-**:

go   get   giggle   goggle   bag   bog

The other is 'soft': *gentle   giant   legend   engine*

The *soft* **g** can also be spelt with a **-j-**:
jump   jacket   jelly   enjoy   object

Warning! There's a **d** before the **g** in:

fudge   edge   ridge   dodge   badge
judge   ledge   midge   lodge

But not in:

age   page   huge   stooge   large   barge

Can you see a rule here? (It's all to do with the vowels.)

kiss and cuddle
consonants **k s**

The letter **-c-** can also be hard, **k**, or soft, **s**

Soft in: *ceiling   circle   cellar   place   face   pencil*
Hard in: *call   coal   cuddle   uncle   picnic   traffic*

c is soft before some letters and not others. Use a dictionary to
investigate when **c** is soft and when it's hard.

The *hard* **c** sound can also be spelt **k**:

kiss   kick   keep   kind   kitchen   kitten   kangaroo   kebab
book   took   shook   make   take   like   spike   woke   spoke
ink   think   thank   monkey   donkey   ask   flask   risk   whisk

or **-ck**, especially after *short vowels*:
back   track   block   shock   stuck   truck   lick   pick

Find out if **ck** is ever the *onset* of a word or syllable.
(Onset is explained on page 9.)

hiss and buzz

consonants *s z*

The letter **s** has two main sounds: *hissing* **s**, **s** and *buzzing* **s**, **z**.

s you can hear in: *slip   slide   this   bus   rocks   socks*
z you can hear in: *is   was   his   hers   dogs   frogs*

s at the *end* of a word always hisses after **-ck** and *buzzes* after **-g**. See if you can find out any more facts, like this, about **s**.

Hissing **s** and soft **c** are the same sound, as you can tell from these homophones:

sell/cell   seller/cellar   ceiling/sealing   sent/cent

There are some other ways, too, to spell **s**, especially at the ends of words and syllables:

Often, after a *short vowel*, the **s** is doubled:
miss   toss   cross   mess   less   fuss   bossy   crossly

Often, after a *long vowel*, you find **-ce**:
place   face   ice   twice   sauce   force   piece   police   juice

and after **-n-**:
prince   mince   once   pounce   chance   dance   experience

-se usually spells **z**:
cheese   please   choose   lose   fuse
rise   surprise   chose   suppose   pause   applause

But watch out for:
chase   case   goose   loose   horse   crease
dense   sense   rinse   else   false   pulse

Buzzing **s** can also be spelt with a **z** or **-zz**:
zoo   zip   hazy   lazy   fizz   buzz
nozzle   guzzle

or **-ze**:
maze   craze   sneeze   freeze   snooze

fish and chips
consonants *sh ch*

ch spells the consonant in
chips   chops   chicken   chunks

After a single *short vowel* it often teams up with **t-**:

itch   stitch   pitch   ditch   witch*   watch
patch   catch   snatch   clutch   fetch   sketch   stretch

 rich   which*   much   such

After *double vowels* and *consonants*, the **t** drops out:

each   teach   poach   arch   search   pouch   touch   torch
lunch   munch   belch   bench   wrench   stench   launch   inch

-sh- spells the consonant in   *fish   shop   ship   crash   splash*

At the beginning or end of a word it always spelt **sh**, except for a few words that have come from French, like:

chef   chassis   chalet   champagne

and  *sugar*

But in the middle of words, the spelling is likely to be **-ti-** or **-si-** especially if it is followed by **-on**:

station   nation   motion   lotion   caution   portion
addition   subtraction   action   fraction
collection   section   friction   mention   attention

tension   pension   extension   diversion
passion   mission   expression   impression

cushion   fashion

Listen, too, for the **sh** in

special   official   vicious   delicious
ferocious   anxious   ocean

How is it spelt in these words?

double trouble
consonant *l*

Many words end with the letters **-le**. They spell the sound *l*.
l is a peculiar consonant, because it can be a syllable by itself, without any particular vowel sound.

*table   stable   apple   wobble   bottle   uncle   angle   tangle
double   trouble   example   crumble   juggle   rustle   wrestle*

The same sound can be spelt **-al**, but you don't hear the **a** . . .
final   legal   local   mammal   metal   national   pedal   royal

. . . and with **-el**, but you can't hear the **e**:

tunnel   towel   vowel   level   barrel   label   model   parcel

In a few words the spelling is **-il**:

council   evil   fossil   lentil   nostril   pencil   pupil

And in a very few it is **-ol**:

carol   petrol   symbol

rough stuff
consonant *f*

The phoneme *f* can be spelt in a few different ways.
Look and listen for it in these words:

*fold   fly   figure   father   face   force   fascinate
leaf   thief   roof   spoof   knife   safe   often   after*

stuff   cliff   afford   daffodil   different   waffle   snuffle

*graph   telegraph   paragraph   physical   phrase   phoneme   photograph   sphere
alphabet   apostrophe   dolphin   elephant*

rough   tough   enough   cough   trough   laugh

There are four spellings for *f* given here. Investigate where each of them can be used in the word – beginning, middle, or end.

Making it plural

There are several different ways to make a noun plural. The *regular* way to make a noun plural is just to put **-s** on the end:

animal ⇨ *animals*   *cat* ⇨ *cats*

But . . . if it ends in **-s** already, add **-es**:

bus ⇨ *buses*   *glass* ⇨ *glasses*   *dress* ⇨ *dresses*

If it ends in **-x** or **-z**, **-ch**, or **-sh**, also add **-es**:

fox ⇨ *foxes*	*tax* ⇨ *taxes*	*buzz* ⇨ *buzzes*
peach ⇨ *peaches*	*stitch* ⇨ *stitches*	*watch* ⇨ *watches*
dish ⇨ *dishes*	*bush* ⇨ *bushes*	*flash* ⇨ *flashes*

If it ends in a *single* **-f** or **-fe**, you may need to change the ending to **-ves**:

leaf ⇨ *leaves*	*loaf* ⇨ *loaves*	*half* ⇨ *halves*
shelf ⇨ *shelves*	*life* ⇨ *lives*	*knife* ⇨ *knives*

But not in: *chiefs   beliefs   dwarfs   proofs   roofs*

If a word ends in a **consonant** then **-y**, change the **-y** to **-ies**:

fly ⇨ *flies*	*spy* ⇨ *spies*	*reply* ⇨ *replies*
party ⇨ *parties*	*baby* ⇨ *babies*	*opportunity* ⇨ *opportunities*

Why is *days* the plural of *day* and *boys* the plural of *boy* and *chimneys* the plural of *chimney*?

If the ending is **-o**, you will just have to remember the spelling, or look it up in a dictionary. Some have **-es** plurals, like:

potatoes   tomatoes   volcanoes   echoes   heroes   mosquitoes

Some have plain **-s** plurals, like:

pianos   radios   photos   kilos   dynamos

Quite a lot of nouns have *irregular* plurals. These are some important ones:

man	*woman*	*child*	*person*	*foot*	*tooth*	*mouse*
⇩	⇩	⇩	⇩	⇩	⇩	⇩
men	*women*	*children*	*people*	*feet*	*teeth*	*mice*

Adding -ed -ing -er -est

Often these endings can be added to the word, without any changes:

push ⇨ *pushed* ⇨ *pushing*   *hard* ⇨ *harder* ⇨ *hardest*

But . . . words which end with silent **-e** usually lose the **e** first:

hope ⇨ *hoped* ⇨ *hoping*   *safe* ⇨ *safer* ⇨ *safest*
smile ⇨ *smiled* ⇨ *smiling*   *wide* ⇨ *wider* ⇨ *widest*
use ⇨ *using* ⇨ *used*   *rude* ⇨ *ruder* ⇨ *rudest*

Remember one-syllable words with a *short vowel* and a *single consonant*:

stop ⇨ *stopped* ⇨ *stopping*   *hot* ⇨ *hotter* ⇨ *hottest*
jog ⇨ *jogged* ⇨ *jogging*   *sad* ⇨ *sadder* ⇨ *saddest*

Be careful with words that end in **-y**:

If there is a consonant before the **y**, change the **y** to **i** before **-ed**, **-er**, **-est**:

fry ⇨ *fried* ⇨ *frying*   *dry* ⇨ *drier* ⇨ *driest*
worry ⇨ *worried* ⇨ *worrying*   *happy* ⇨ *happier* ⇨ *happiest*
copy ⇨ *copied* ⇨ *copying*   *funny* ⇨ *funnier* ⇨ *funniest*

If there is a vowel before the **-y**, then just add the suffix:
play ⇨ *played* ⇨ *playing*   *annoy* ⇨ *annoyed* ⇨ *annoying*
 obey ⇨ *obeyed* ⇨ *obeying*
But these *don't* obey: *say* ⇨ *said*   *pay* ⇨ *paid*   *lay* ⇨ *laid*

If a word ends in **-ie**, change this to **-y** before adding **-ing**
lie ⇨ *lied* ⇨ *lying*   *tie* ⇨ *tied* ⇨ *tying*   *die* ⇨ *died* ⇨ *dying*

Some verbs don't end in **-ed** but have completely irregular spellings.

These are some:

take ⇨ *took*   *shake* ⇨ *shook*   *stand* ⇨ *stood*
hide ⇨ *hid*   *bite* ⇨ *bit*   *light* ⇨ *lit*   *do* ⇨ *did*
sell ⇨ *sold*   *tell* ⇨ *told*   *hold* ⇨ *held*   *go* ⇨ *went*
shoot ⇨ *shot*   *get* ⇨ *got*   *lose* ⇨ *lost*   *come* ⇨ *came*
sleep ⇨ *slept*   *creep* ⇨ *crept*   *feel* ⇨ *felt*
fly ⇨ *flew*   *throw* ⇨ *threw*   *draw* ⇨ *drew*   *know* ⇨ *knew*
break ⇨ *broke*   *wake* ⇨ *woke*   *write* ⇨ *wrote*   *see* ⇨ *saw*
begin ⇨ *began*   *run* ⇨ *ran*

Prefixes

Prefixes are bits that are added in front of the main part of a word, called the **root**.

For example: *dis*appear   *re*appear   *pre*pare *com*pare

These are some of the prefixes you should know how to spell:

un-	*uncover unpack unload undo* *untidy unhappy unfair unnecessary*
dis-	*discover disappointed disagree disgust*
re-	*recover report refresh reply*
de-	*defend decide depend delighted*
pre-	*preview pretend prepare prehistoric*
mis-	*mistake misuse misunderstand misbehave*
non-	*nonsense non-stick non-stop non-fiction*
ex-	*excuse explode explore express*
anti-	*antifreeze anticlockwise anticlimax*
in-	This prefix has four different spellings *in-* *im-* *il-* *ir-* *incorrect inhuman inescapable intake* *impossible impatient immovable immediate* *illegal illegible illustrate* *irregular irresistible irresponsible*

Use a dictionary to investigate when to use each of these prefixes.

disappear   *reappear*

Suffixes

Suffixes are bits added on to the end of a root word.

On page 29 you can find out how to add the suffixes **-ed**, **-ing**, **-er**, **-est**.
Here are some more useful suffixes with their root words.
Notice that you may have to change the end of the root when you add a suffix.

-ly	slow slowly	full fully	happy happily
-al	nation national	post postal	practice practical
-ary	prime primary	second secondary	imagine imaginary
-ive	expense expensive	act active	secret secretive
-tion	inspect inspection	attend attention	deceive deception
-sion	decide decision	televise television	admit admission
-ful	hope hopeful	fear fearful	plenty plentiful
-less	hope hopeless	fear fearless	mercy merciless
-hood	likely likelihood	child childhood	neighbour neighbourhood
-ness	good goodness	ill illness	busy business
-ment	agree agreement	state statement	pay payment

Words you need to know

a	help	pull	above	goes	started
about	her	push	across	gone	still
after	here	put	almost	great	stopped
again	him	ran	along	half	such
all	his	said	also	happy	suddenly
am	home	saw	always	head	sure
an	house	school	animals	heard	swimming
and	how	seen	any	high	think
another	I	she	around	I'm	those
are	if	should	asked	important	thought
as	in	sister	baby	inside	through
at	is	so	balloon	jumped	today
away	it	some	before	knew	together
back	jump	take	began	know	told
ball	just	than	being	lady	tries
be	last	that	below	leave	turn
because	laugh	the	better	light	turned
bed	like	their	between	might	under
been	little	them	birthday	money	until
big	live	then	both	morning	upon
boy	lived	there	brother	mother	used
but	look	these	brought	much	walk
by	love	they	can't	near	walked
call	made	this	change	never	walking
called	make	three	children	number	watch
came	man	time	clothes	often	while
can	many	to	coming	only	white
cat	may	too	didn't	opened	whole
come	me	took	different	other	why
could	more	tree	does	outside	window
dad	mum	two	don't	own	without
day	must	up	during	paper	woke
did	my	us	earth	place	woken
dig	name	very	every	right	word
do	new	want	eyes	round	work
dog	next	was	father	second	world
don't	night	water	first	show	write
door	no	way	follow	sister	year
down	not	we	following	small	young
for	now	went	found	something	
from	of	were	friends	sometimes	
get	off	what	garden	sound	
girl	old	when			
go	on	where			
going	once	who			
good	one	will			
got	or	with			
had	our	would			
half	out	yes			
has	over	you			
have	people	your			
he	play				